Prepping:

Complete Reference About Creating Your Own Bug Out Bag

The trademarks that are used are without any consent, and the publication of the trademark is without permission or backing by the trademark owner. All trademarks and brands within this book are for clarifying purposes only and are the owned by the owners themselves, not affiliated with this document.

Table of Contents

Introduction

The evacuation notice rings out, and you have to get going. You don't have time to go through your house or to make sure you have everything. You have to grab and you have to get out.

You don't know where you are going, you just have to get somewhere safe, and you have to get there now. So what are you going to grab? There's only a few seconds for you to get out the door, and you have to be on the road in a matter of minutes. No time to go through anything, no time to get ready, just grab and go.

Of course, you grab your bug-out bag. You know that no matter where you are headed, you have enough in your bag to keep you comfortable for the next few days. You might have to be on the road, you might have to be in close quarters with other people, and you might have to keep moving, but no matter what, you are going to have the necessities you need to stay comfortable during this time.

Or do you?

Do you have one of these handy little kits sitting where you can grab it at any second? Do you have what you need to hit the road if you are suddenly told you have to do it? Are you ready to head out into the great unknown?

If you don't feel like you are, you are not alone. So many people need a lot of time to get ready, or they are forced to leave with nothing but the clothes on their backs. I don't want this to be you. I want you to be able to leave at any time you need to, and be ready to face the days to come.

With this book, I am going to show you how to put together your very own bug-out bag, and make sure you stock it with all of the necessities you are going to need to survive anywhere you need to for three days. I know it sounds scary, but there is a lot of comfort in knowing you have what you need with you.

Remove some of the worry you are going to feel by putting together one of these kits, and rest assured you have what it takes to push through any disaster you are faced with.

You will be so glad you did.

Chapter 1 – Bug-Out Bag Overview: What Is It?

In this modern day in which we live, a lot of people are really in to survival and survival preparation. There are a lot of people out there that are ready for anything... no matter what it is. Of course, in the modern world we live in, a lot of the natural disasters that were once a surprise threat aren't so bad anymore, but it's still a good idea to be ready.

These days, we may not be able to avoid the disasters, but we do have more of an idea of when they are going to strike.

Regardless of where you live, you are at risk of a natural disaster, and having to suddenly be evacuated. You may be going about your day without a care in the world, when suddenly you are told you have to leave, and you have no idea of when you are going to be back.

When things like this happen, you have to be ready to go. You have to have that emergency kit ready to go at any time... and that is where the bug-out bag comes in.

If you have never heard of one of these survival kits before, you may be wondering what on earth they are, and how they got their name. Well, the answer is simple on both accounts.

These bags stem out of the old war days, in which soldiers had to be ready to evacuate and move at any given moment. As such, they were instructed to have kits set up that they could use to survive on the go for a standard of three days.

The length of time each kit could support an individual varied, and still does to an extent, from the twenty-four hour kit to kits that can last an entire week. The longer the kit is supposed to last, the more supplies are needed.

As a general rule of thumb, however, these bags are meant to last a total of seventy-two hours, or three days. The reason for this is based on the rule set forth by the disaster relief centers which state that you should be ready to fend for yourself for three days in the event it takes them that long to reach you after a natural disaster.

Through the course of time, these bags have held different names, but their general purpose has been the same, and that is to help maintain your comfort for a period of three days

Now, what you put in these bags is going to be based on where you live first and foremost, followed by your own special needs and even your own preferences.

For example, if you live in the South or in a hot and dessert kind of region, you are going to need vastly different things in your bag than if you live in an area that is prone to blizzards or flooding.

In addition, you need to make sure your bug-out bag is current on the time of year it is. Many places have different kinds of threats depending on the time of year it is, and they are going to need different supplies based on this time of year. If you are in the North, you are going to need to pack things that are warm in the winter months, and cooler supplies to protect against heat stroke if you are in the summer months.

No matter where you are or what time of year it is, there are going to be staples that you will put in your kit. These are things you will need... or may need... no matter what else is going on.

These things include medical supplies, food, water (or a way to get water) communication, and things along these lines. In the chapters to come, we are going to take a look at the specific things you should keep in your bug-out bag, the most effective ways you can put together your bug-out bag, and ways you can use your bug-out bag when you are in a situation where you need it.

The better prepared you are, the better off you are going to be in a disaster. This is going to take some time and effort to put together, and you may need to spread out putting your kit together over time, but when you finally have your kit together, you are going to be ready for anything that comes your way.

And the peace of mind that provides is going to be worth more than any kit you could possibly buy.

Chapter 2 – Getting Started With Your Bag

If you decide to shop around for bug-out kits, you are going to see a wide range of different kinds available. As I said in the last chapter, you are going to find a range of time that these kits are meant to last for, and that is going to directly affect what is in the bag and how much it costs.

Of course, if you were buy one of these kits, you are going to get the standard things the companies put into each one. This is going to have some benefits, but a lot of drawbacks as you have no control over what in particular you need in your bag.

Which, of course, means you are going to end up with things that you don't need, or possibly won't use, or you are going to end up not having things you do need or could have used if you had the option of including it.

My point, however, isn't so much what is included inside the premade kits as what these kits are included in

In other words... what is the container that your supplies come in? A standard bug-out bag is a small pack that usually has a clear case for the front. This shows you what is inside the bag before you get one, so you know what you are getting for your supplies.

But, if you are making your own bag, you may be wondering what it is you should include, and what it is you should put your supplies in. If you are going to make a small bag, you can use virtually anything you want to put your supplies in. If you know where your things are, and you know what you put inside it, it really doesn't matter what you put these supplies in.

Again, if you spend any time online you are going to find a wide range of different options people have chosen to put their supplies in. Some opt for small bags with minimal things in them, almost like lunch boxes. Others prefer backpacks or larger sacks they can fit more into besides the basic supplies they need for the moment.

However you decide to pack your things, make sure you are able to grab your bag in a hurry, and that you are able to carry it with you over a distance. Some people make the mistake of packing a bag that is too large to carry, and when they are evacuated, they have to leave on foot, and they aren't able to take their bag with them because it's simply too big.

To solve this problem, you can always pack more than one bag if you need. It's better to have two smaller bug-out bags you can take with you than one large one that is too big to lift.

Either way, make sure that your bag isn't too heavy for you to carry over long distances... you never know how far you are going to have to walk.

Or, if you are in some situations, you might have to fit into a bus or some sort of other rescue craft with a lot of other people, and if that is the case, you may not be allowed to carry things that are very big.

You want your supplies to fit snugly into whatever case you decide to bring, and you want to be as efficient as possible with each one. The more you can fit into a smaller sized compartment, the better... as long as you can carry it.

If you would rather, split as much as you can comfortably carry between two bags, and you are going to be ready for anything.

I recommend you practice carrying your bag (or something that is equivalent to your bag) over a distance until you are really used to carrying it, and used to carrying it for a distance. The more you can carry... and the faster you can carry it... the better off you are in the long run.

Practice until you are able to pick it up and be ready to go in under five minutes or less. More often than not you are going to have more notice than just that, but it never hurts to be ready to go faster than what you need to be.

In addition to being able to carry your bag over a distance, and being able to fit a lot of things in your bag, you need to know what you have in there.

When it comes to gathering supplies, you may get so caught up packing things into your bag that you forget to make a list of the things you have in there. This is going to make it difficult to know what you should keep an eye out for, and if there is anything else you may be forgetting

As I have already said, depending on the season, you are going to need different things in your bag. With this in mind, you can either set up two bags... one for each of the seasons you are facing... or you can keep a list of the items you keep in your bag and adjust what you have in there accordingly.

There's nothing wrong with cleaning out your bag every few months to check what you have in there, and to make sure you are up to date with what you do want to have in there. Make a list depending on the time of year that it is, and you are going to always know what you have and what you need, or what you need to keep an eye out for.

Now, when it comes to what actually goes into your pack, you may feel intimidated by what you read online. Of course there are the basics, but if you do any sort of research on the topic, you are going to find that there are people out there that spend months if not years putting their packs together.

But, no matter how much you put in your bag, you are always going to find something better, or something more efficient to keep in there. You might think you have the perfect bag, then you read somewhere a bunch of other things you need to include, or that you shouldn't have something that you decided to have.

When it really comes down to it, you have to decide for yourself what you want to have in there, as long as you reach the same basic supplies you need to make it through a few days. In the next few chapters, we are going to take a look at what these things are, and what you should specifically aim to keep in your bag depending on your area.

Don't worry if you find something on the list you don't want to have, or if you don't see something on the list that you think you should have. There is room for modification and personalization.

As long as you have the basic things in your bag, you are able to get to your bag quickly, and carry it for long distances, and you know what you have in your bag, you are going to be ready for any kind of disaster that comes your way.

Now, let's get into the list of must-haves you need to include in your bug-out bag.

Chapter 3 – Stuffing the Stocking: What to Put in Your Bag

If you shop around to find the bag you want to keep your supplies in, you may end up spending a lot of time weighing your options. After all, as we saw in the last chapter, there are several things you want to consider before you get your bag, and there are several things you want to do once you have it.

Of course, once you see the bag you want, you know it. And, once you get this bad, you are ready for the fun part... stuffing it.

When it comes to the things you put in your bag, you are going to have a lot of excitement. Of course, when it comes to the things you put in your bag, you have so many options you can choose from it can also get to be incredibly overwhelming.

There are two things you have to keep in mind when you are deciding what to put in your bag, and they are:

1. **Think through what you are going to need when you are on the road, and**

2. **You don't need everything you are told you are going to need by those who are online**

Of course, there are some excellent ideas by many people who are posting online, but if you take a look at the things you could potentially put in your bag, you are going to find lists of hundreds of items.

Before you head to the store and grab a hundred things to stuff into your bag, you have to genuinely ask yourself how many things you really do need to survive for a few days on the road. When you think of it this way, you are going to realize how few things you really do need to make it through a few days.

Food, water, shelter, and basic supplies are really all you need to get through a few days. Of course there are a number of things that are going to make these few days easier, but when it comes down to the bare necessities, you really don't need that many things.

Let's slow down for a moment, and take a look at each of these basic things you need. Make your list out of these things, and add in just a few things you personally want to bring along with you. We'll take a deeper look at these things in the chapters to come, but for now, we are going to worry about the basics.

- **Food** – this can be a bit of a challenge. When you think of the food you are going to take in a preparedness kit, you want to plan for something that is quick and easy.

    Thankfully, there are tons of options when it comes to backpack meals, protein bars and shakes, and dehydrated foods. If you can stock your bag with food that is ready to open and eat, or if you only need to add water, you are on the right track.

- **Water** – when it comes to water, you are once again going to have to be creative. Of course, you can keep water bottles in your bag, but you have to be careful to think about how many water bottles you are going to need to last three days. This can be a surprising amount, and can make it hard for you to move your bag quickly or over long distances.

  A better option is to pack a water bottle with water, and to pack a water bottle with a water purification system. This is going to enable you to clean and use any water you find along the way.

- **Shelter** – you would be amazed at how small tents can fold these days. Whether you choose a small pup tent for yourself, or if you choose a tarp that you can set up as a form of shelter, you have to have something that you can fold and keep in your pack, and something that you can quickly unfold and set up or take back down when you need to.

- **Clothes** – the clothing you take should be basic, a change of clothing is plenty. You don't need to pack a lot of things here, because you really only need it when the clothing you have is ruined or too cold. Remember that this is only for three days, and you can put up with a lot for three days.

- **Medical supplies** – make sure you have both pain killers, antiseptic, butterfly bandages or stitches, and normal bandages. It's hard for you to overpack when it comes to the medical supplies, whether you are the one that needs it, or if you end up around someone else who does. Make sure you pack generously your medical supplies, and you are going to be fine.

- **The basics for day to day living** – the rest of the basics include such things as matches, fire starter, perhaps something small to use for cooking, a flashlight with batteries, a pocket knife that actually works, and some form of communication

Overall, you are going to have flexibility on what you should pack for the extras, but make sure you have this list in your pack, no matter what. We are going to look further into the last part of the list in the next chapter so you know for sure what you should have depending on where you live, as well as some options you have for other supplies.

But, if these are the only things you put in your bag, you are going to be better off than most of the unprepared people on the road.

Chapter 4 – Diving Into the Extras

Only you know where you live and the various kinds of natural disasters that you could face in that area. Use your head, or search for what the people who live in similar places have.

If you are in somewhere hot, you need to make sure you have plenty of water supplies, and that you have clothing that will protect you from the sun and heat if you end up outdoors. If you are in a blizzarding kind of area, you want to keep warm clothing on hand, or ways to make fire.

But perhaps the most important extra thing you can keep in your pack is a radio, or some kind of phone

You need to be careful when it comes to the electronics you can keep… radios may not work in certain areas, or cell service may be down in your area, making it difficult to get a hold of emergency people or loved ones. To combat this, you need to keep a radio on hand that you can operate through batteries, and keep some sort of phone on hand you can get cards for.

This way, no matter what is going on with the cell service, you are going to have some way to get a hold of other people in your area, even if it's just to keep up with the news and where the emergency crews are.

Check in often to see what is going on in the area, and to check to see if there is further danger you have to be aware of. The more you know, the better off you are going to be.

When it comes to such things as weapons or knives, you can again choose based on your location and the problems you are going to face

Also check to see if you need some kind of permit to carry the weapon. If you are in a true survival situation, you may not be worried about such things, but if you are in a controlled evacuation, you are going to be more concerned with the regulations and permits you need to have.

It's always better to do things by the letter when your state requires it, because you never know what kind of situation you are going to be in exactly. The more you can keep things running smoothly, the easier it is going to be to get through the time you are in.

As far as knives go, you want something that is multi-functional. This is going to make it a lot easier for you to be ready for anything that comes your way.

For example:

If you only have a small pocket knife, you aren't going to be well prepared for a branch that has fallen across the road and needs to be moved. If you only have a large knife suitable for cutting trees, you aren't going to have what you need if you need to tend to a smaller, more detailed kind of cut.

To remedy this, you need to either pack more than one kind of knife, or you are going to have to pack a knife that you can convert from one kind of knife to another. Give it some thought to determine for sure what you need, then shop around for the best deals.

Along with anything else, make sure you have what is most important to you as well

You might not be able to pack everything, but if there's that photo you simply must have, or you need that letter your loved one wrote you when they were away, pack it up.

You never know what is going to happen during times like these, and you may not have much to come back to in extreme cases. When things like this happen, you are going to need something to keep your mood up and keep you going.

Even if it's something as small as a stuffed animal you care about, make sure you bring it along with you. You never know how much things like these can matter until you are in these kinds of situations.

Chapter 5 – Final Preparations

As with anything like this, some things you are going to have to figure out when it happens, but there are still things you can prepare for in advance that are going to make you better able to handle it when it does happen.

For starters, make sure you are mentally ready to face something like this. You may think you are ready, but few people actually know what it is going to be like before they are in the situation, and while you may personally be ready to handle it, a lot of others may not be, and you may end up being that rock they need.

When natural disasters happen, you have to remain calm, and know that what is important is that you made it out and that your loved ones are safe. Everything else in life can be replaced, and no matter how bad things look, you are going to be able to get them back with time.

Get a plan in place so you are ready for it when it does happen

Know where your bag is, where your things are, and how to get them quickly. Make sure you know where you are meeting your loved ones, or where you are headed if such a thing happens.

Grab the things you need, and get going. When evacuations are taking place, there's really no time for you to waste. Gather what you need and get where you need to be without a second thought about what you are leaving behind. If you prepare properly, you are going to leave with the assurance that you have everything, and you aren't forgetting anything.

Remain calm, and do as you are instructed

We all know what we are capable of, but there are times when it is better for you to just do as the professionals tell you, and go where they say. If you are able to help, then by all means, but don't try to be a hero when you are told to do something.

There are times when the most important thing you can do is to do what you are told, and to take care of your own things. Make sure you personally are ready, and when it happens, you are out the door and ready to go.

Your bug-out bag is going to take a lot of stress off of you, so get it ready, and be ready to do your part.

Conclusion

There you have it, everything you need to know to put together your own bug-out bag, and how to assemble one based on what kind of life you live. You might feel nervous packing a bag in case you ever have to evacuate your home, but you shouldn't.

You should be happy for the chance to be able to prepare for anything that could happen, and put the supplies you are going to need in your kit. There is so much more to survival than just being able to find food or have medical supplies. Being able to have access to the little things that matter to you is just as important as anything else you could put in your bug-out bag.

So let this book inspire you to fill your bag with the things that you need to make it through any three days you may be faced with. Sure, you might not have the most comfortable time with the things you have to deal with, but with this kit by your side, you know you have what you need to make it through for a while.

Pack your bug-out bag with confidence, knowing you are going to face the hardship as it comes, and emerge on the other side as though nothing ever happened in the first place.

FREE Bonus Reminder

If you have not grabbed it yet, please go ahead and download your special bonus report *"Preppers Survival Guide. Proven Tactics For Armed Incounters!"*

Simply Click the Button Below

OR **Go to This Page**

http://preppersliving.com/free

BONUS #2: More Free & Discounted Books & Products

Do you want to receive more Free/Discounted Books or Products?

We have a mailing list where we send out our new Books or Products when they go free or with a discount on Amazon. Click on the link below to sign up for Free & Discount Book & Product Promotions.

=> Sign Up for Free & Discount Book & Product Promotions <=

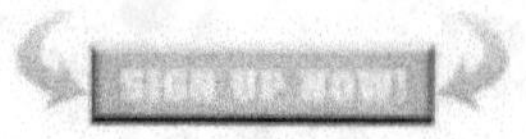

OR Go to this URL

http://zbit.ly/1WBb1Ek